MW01600683

THIS PLANNER BELONGS TO:

_____

_____

COPYRIGHT

All rights reserved. No part of this planner may be reproduced in any form without expressed permission from the publisher, except in the case of brief quotations.

This planner should not be considered a legally binding document. It is recommended you consult with a lawyer to create a formal, legally binding will regarding your desired final wishes and arrangements should you become incapacitated, or upon passing.

The author, publisher, and all those involved in the creation of this workbook, under any and all circumstances, are not considered responsible or liable for any damages that come from its content or purchase. Use of this planner is meant entirely for the benefit of the purchaser in the organization and documentation for end of life wishes and preferences.

It is a good idea to ensure those involved in your end of life planning and arrangements are notified of this document and its location. Important, sensitive and private content such as personal identification information and passwords are included in the following pages, and it is essential this information not become misplaced to avoid the risk of identity theft or misuse of any kind.

The owner and users of this document takes full responsibility for the safekeeping, accuracy, and content upon use. The user agrees this planner is considered an organizational workbook only, in which to record final wishes and desires relevant in the case of incapacitation or upon passing.

© 2021, Peace of Mind and Heart Planners

TABLE OF CONTENTS

INTRODUCTION

Welcome to your Peace of Mind and Heart Planner. This workbook is designed to make life-planning as simple, user-friendly, and stress free as possible.

WARNING:

We have placed humour, sarcasm, and a few naughty words throughout the content of the book for some levity while planning for a serious matter. We hope you enjoy it as much as we did including it!

On a serious note, your Peace of Mind Notebook is a comprehensive, customizable, all-in-one Planner to record your vital information, estate planning, personal wishes, and final messages to loved ones.

It is a valuable gift for those left behind so that they can ensure your instructions are fulfilled accordingly, and to help avoid duress or confusion by preparing in advance.

We have provided plenty of space to customize each section as per your needs, and include additional overflow space if required, plus a section for personal messages to your loved ones.

It is wise to begin with the initial personal identification section first, and then proceed to one chapter at a time, collecting all the documentation and information in advance for efficiency sake.

Remember to update this planner as changes to your circumstances arise, such as new employment, investments, insurance, or adjustments to your personal wishes.

Please note, this planner is not a legal document and should not be considered a formal will.

*Always store this workbook somewhere safe, to prevent sensitive, private information from getting into the wrong hands.

PERSONAL INFORMATION

My Legal Name

Favorite Nickname

Least Favorite Nickname That Pissed Me Off

Address

Mailbox or P.O. Box Number (The one you're allowed to know about)

Mailbox Location

Key Location

Primary Phone Numbers

Phone Number/s I Never Told You About

Just Kidding... No, Really

4

Family Members and Dependents

Spouse's Name / Maiden Name

_____

_____

Spouse's Nickname When I Wanted to Have My Way _____

Spouse's Nickname When I Wanted to Piss Him / Her Off _____

Children's Names	Favorite Nicknames

Grandchildren's Names	Favorite Nicknames

All Dependents Legal Names

Pet Nicknames

Pets Names

Pet Nicknames

Notes

Siblings Names   Favorite Nicknames

_____

_____

_____

_____

_____

Mother's Name / Maiden Name

_____

_____

Father's Name

_____

_____

Ex-Spouse's Name

_____

_____

My Favorite 'Not So Nice' Nickname for Ex-Spouse _____

How Great It Felt to Use It, Scale of 1 – 10: (1 = Low, 10 = High) _____

Notes and Random Vent

_____

_____

_____

_____

AT THE TIME OF PASSING

Please Contact the Following People Immediately Upon My Passing or Incapacity

Spouse / Partner

Name

Contact Information

Notes

Healthcare Power of Attorney Agent

Name

Contact Information

Notes

Executor

Name

Contact Information

Notes

Person I Wish Was Taking My Place

(Fiction, Non-Fiction, Politician, Royal Dumb Ass, Etc.)

1st Place Prize

2nd Place Prize

Please Contact the Following Family, Friends, Associates, or Paid Actors upon My Passing

Name

Contact Information

Relationship

Name

Contact Information

Relationship

Name

Contact Information

Relationship

Name

Contact Information

Relationship

Name

Contact Information

Relationship

Name

Contact Information

Relationship

Name

Contact Information

Relationship

Notes

Please Contact the Following People

Name

Contact Information

Relationship

Name

Contact Information

Relationship

Name

Contact Information

Relationship

Name

Contact Information

Relationship

Name

Contact Information

Relationship

Name

Contact Information

Relationship

Name

Contact Information

Relationship

Notes

Please Contact the Following People

Name

Contact Information

Relationship

Name

Contact Information

Relationship

Name

Contact Information

Relationship

Name

Contact Information

Relationship

Name

Contact Information

Relationship

Name

Contact Information

Relationship

Name

Contact Information

Relationship

Notes

Please Contact the Following People

Name

Contact Information

Relationship

Name

Contact Information

Relationship

Name

Contact Information

Relationship

Name

Contact Information

Relationship

Name

Contact Information

Relationship

Name

Contact Information

Relationship

Name

Contact Information

Relationship

Notes

Please Contact the Following People

Name

Contact Information

Relationship

Name

Contact Information

Relationship

Name

Contact Information

Relationship

Name

Contact Information

Relationship

Name

Contact Information

Relationship

Name

Contact Information

Relationship

Name

Contact Information

Relationship

Notes

Place of Worship: Church, Synagogue, Etc.

Name #1

Contact Information

Name #2

Contact Information

Notes

Lawyer #1 Corruption Level / 10 = ?

Name

Contact Information

Notes

Lawyer #2 Corruption Level / 10 = ?

Name

Contact Information

Notes

Estate Planner

(If he/she accepts monetary tips for this position, fire and replace immediately)

Name

Contact Information

Notes

Business Employer / Associate (Assuming you were employable)

Company and Agent Name _____

Contact Information _____

Business Employer / Associate (If the first time you don't succeed, try, try again)

Company and Agent Name _____

Contact Information _____

Business Employer / Associate (...and again)

Company and Agent Name _____

Contact Information _____

Financial Advisor #1 (Did you take the advice?)

Company and Agent Name _____

Contact Information _____

Financial Advisor #2 (Did you give him / her advice?)

Company and Agent Name _____

Contact Information _____

Accountant (If he / she cannot count to 10, you have a problem)

Company and Agent Name _____

Contact Information _____

Notes _____

Health Care Provider – Medical (Sorry, not enough room to bitch about healthcare here)

Company and Agent Name

Contact Information

Health Care Provider – Dental

Company and Agent Name

Contact Information

Health Care Provider – Vision

Company and Agent Name

Contact Information

Health Care Provider – Other

Company and Agent Name

Contact Information

Veterinarian

Company and Agent Name

Contact Information

Veterinarian

Company and Agent Name

Contact Information

Notes

Other

Name

Contact Information

Name

Contact Information

Name

Contact Information

Name

Contact Information

Name

Contact Information

Name

Contact Information

Name

Contact Information

Name

Contact Information

Notes

Contact Information – Notes

(Bitch Fest Welcome Here, Plenty of Room Now)

FUNERAL ARRANGEMENTS

Funeral Arrangements Contact Person

Location

Contact Information

Church, Synagogue, Other

Name of Priest, Rabbi, Other

Contact Information

Funeral Home

Address

Contact Information

Cemetery or Crematorium

Plot / Address

Contact Information

Funeral Insurance Policy

Company Name

Contact Information

Notes and Who I'd Like to Return as Next Lifetime

Burial

Headstone Details

Cremation

Ashes to be spread

Obituary

Please Include the Following

Notes

(And what I'd really like to say on my headstone, or do with my ashes)

Funeral Arrangements - Celebration of Life Services

Please Include the Following Personal Message to My Loved Ones (Now is the time to express yourself, it's safe to do so!)

Additional Instructions

Funeral Arrangements - Notes

Funeral Arrangements – Notes

ASSETS OVERVIEW – WHAT MY LOVED ONES CAN EXPECT

Personal Residence Address

Note: Please see will for detailed instructions and division of assets

_____

_____

PO Box Location and Address

_____

_____

Partner / Co-Owner Names

_____

_____

Contact Information

_____

_____

Legal Will Location and Instructions for Division of Assets

_____

_____

_____

_____

My Family and Friends Are My Assets, Just Give Everything Away! Just Kidding Scale = ? /10

_____

_____

_____

Keys Location and Miscellaneous Instructions

Alarm and Security Information

(The one before I changed It so the police bust your ass)

Utilities Warranties and Documentation Location

Upkeep Information and Document Location (Gardener, Etc.)

Notes

Real Estate Investment - Second Property Address

(If this is blank I don't have a second home and just wanted you to get all excited)

Type of Property (Residential / Commercial)

PO Box Location and Address

Partner / Co-Owner Names

Contact Information

Legal Documentation Location and Instructions

Keys Location and Miscellaneous Instructions
(I forget, sorry)

Alarm and Security Information
(Forgot this too, good luck with that)

Utilities Warranties and Documentation Location

Upkeep Information and Document Location (Gardener, Etc.)

Notes

Vehicle List: Car, Motorcycle, Recreation Vehicle, Snowmobile, Etc.

(The legal one's)

Vehicle _____

Year/Make/Model _____

_____

VIN – ID _____

Ownership Documentation Location _____

Lease / Load Information _____

Keys Location _____

Notes _____

_____

_____

_____

Vehicle _____

Year/Make/Model _____

_____

VIN – ID _____

Ownership Documentation Location _____

Lease / Load Information _____

Keys Location _____

Notes _____

_____

_____

_____

Vehicle List:

Vehicle

Year/Make/Model

VIN – ID

Ownership Documentation Location

Lease / Load Information

Keys Location

Notes

Vehicle

Year/Make/Model

VIN – ID

Ownership Documentation Location

Lease / Load Information

Keys Location

Notes

Investments: Stocks, Mutual Funds, and Other

(I invested in myself, good food, good drink, good xxx, nothing to see here)

Type

Location

Account Number

Contact Person

Documentation Location

Notes

Type

Location

Account Number

Contact Person

Documentation Location

Notes

Type

Location

Account Number

Contact Person

Documentation Location

Notes

Investments: Ditto

Type

Location

Account Number

Contact Person

Documentation Location

Notes

Type

Location

Account Number

Contact Person

Documentation Location

Notes

Type

Location

Account Number

Contact Person

Documentation Location

Notes

Investments: Ditto

Type

Location

Account Number

Contact Person

Documentation Location

Notes

Type

Location

Account Number

Contact Person

Documentation Location

Notes

Type

Location

Account Number

Contact Person

Documentation Location

Notes

Insurance Benefits:

(After years of contributing, they sure AF owe me.)

Policy Type

Location

Account Number

Contact Person

Documentation Location

Notes

Policy Type

Location

Account Number

Contact Person

Documentation Location

Notes

Policy Type

Location

Account Number

Contact Person

Documentation Location

Notes

Assets Overview

Insurance Benefits:

Policy Type

Location

Account Number

Contact Person

Documentation Location

Notes

Policy Type

Location

Account Number

Contact Person

Documentation Location

Notes

Policy Type

Location

Account Number

Contact Person

Documentation Location

Notes

Employer Benefits #1

(Cross your fingers it isn't gone with the economy, or go with Musk to Mars)

Name

Account Number

Contact Person

Documentation Location

Notes

Employer Benefits #2

Name

Account Number

Contact Person

Documentation Location

Notes

Employer Benefits #3

Name

Account Number

Contact Person

Documentation Location

Notes

Retirement Benefits

(Same as Above)

Name

Account Number

Contact Person

Documentation Location

Notes

Retirement Benefits #2

Name

Account Number

Contact Person

Documentation Location

Notes

Social Security

Name

Account Number

Contact Person

Documentation Location

Notes

Other: Veteran's Benefits, Etc.

Name

Account Number

Contact Person

Documentation Location

Notes

Other:

Name

Account Number

Contact Person

Documentation Location

Notes

Other:

Name

Account Number

Contact Person

Documentation Location

Notes

Money Owed to Me

(Tell them I say hi)

Name _____

Account Number _____

Contact Person _____

Documentation Location _____

Notes _____

_____

_____

_____

Name _____

Account Number _____

Contact Person _____

Documentation Location _____

Notes _____

_____

_____

_____

Name _____

Account Number _____

Contact Person _____

Documentation Location _____

Notes _____

_____

Personal Items, Jewelry, and Heirlooms

(No fighting please. My shit, my rules!)

Item

Location

Notes

Item

Location

Notes

Item

Location

Notes

Item

Location

Notes

Personal Items, Jewelry, and Heirlooms

Item

Location

Notes

Item

Location

Notes

Item

Location

Notes

Item

Location

Notes

Personal Items, Jewelry, and Heirlooms

Item

Location

Notes

Item

Location

Notes

Item

Location

Notes

Item

Location

Notes

Personal Items, Jewelry, and Heirlooms

Item

Location

Notes

Item

Location

Notes

Item

Location

Notes

Item

Location

Notes

Personal Items, Jewelry, and Heirlooms

Item

Location

Notes

Item

Location

Notes

Item

Location

Notes

Item

Location

Notes

Personal Items, Jewelry, and Heirlooms

Item

Location

Notes

Item

Location

Notes

Item

Location

Notes

Item

Location

Notes

Storage Company #1

Name

Address

Key Location or Combination Number

Storage Company #2

Name

Address

Key Location or Combination Number

Notes, Instructions, and Personal Grudges

BUSINESS INFORMATION

Business Details

(See, that's why I wasn't employed, I had my own freaking business!)

Business Name

Business Type

Address

Landlord Name

Contact Information

Lease Documentation Location

Partner / Co-Owner Name

Contact Information

Partner / Co-Owner Name

Contact Information

Partner / Co-Owner Name

Contact Information

Partner / Co-Owner Name

Contact Information

Keys Location

Notes

Associates, Employees, and Contractors

(...Who actually liked me, the others are in the back yard)

Name

Contact Information

Name

Contact Information

Name

Contact Information

Name

Contact Information

Name

Contact Information

Name

Contact Information

Name

Contact Information

Name

Contact Information

Notes

Business Information

Name

Contact Information

Name

Contact Information

Name

Contact Information

Name

Contact Information

Name

Contact Information

Name

Contact Information

Name

Contact Information

Name

Contact Information

Notes

Bank Name

Address

Contact Information

Business Bank Account Number

Business Bank Account Number

Credit Card Number

Username / PIN

Credit Card Number

Username / PIN

Documentation Location

Notes

What I'd Like to Say to Them

Bank Name

Address

Contact Information

Business Bank Account Number

Business Bank Account Number

Credit Card Number

Username / PIN

Credit Card Number

Username / PIN

Documentation Location

Notes

What I'd Like to Say to Them

Accountant Name

Contact Information

Performance /10   Trustworthiness / 10

Lawyer

Contact Information

Performance /10   Trustworthiness / 10

Insurance Agency / Agent

Contact Information

Performance /10   Trustworthiness / 10

Notes on Income, Royalties, Key Accounts, and Other Shit

Business Website Name

Hosting Provider

Username and Password

Website Developer Name

Contact Information

Documentation Location

Online Income Stream #1

Online Income Stream #2

Partner / Co-Owner Name

Contact Information

Partner / Co-Owner Name

Contact Information

Partner / Co-Owner Name

Contact Information

Business Email Address Name

Username and Password

Business Email Address Name

Username and Password

Business Email Address Name

Username and Password

Notes

Notes:

Instructions for Domain Name Renewal, Hosting, Expenses, and Partners to Trust / Not Trust

Social Media

(My Private Shit You Could Never Log Into....Until Now)

Name

Username and Password

Name

Username and Password

Name

Username and Password

Name

Username and Password

Name

Username and Password

Name

Username and Password

Name

Username and Password

Name

Username and Password

Name

Username and Password

Name

Username and Password

Accounts

Name

Username and Password

Name

Username and Password

Name

Username and Password

Name

Username and Password

Name

Username and Password

Name

Username and Password

Name

Username and Password

Name

Username and Password

Name

Username and Password

Name

Username and Password

Accounts

Name

Username and Password

Name

Username and Password

Name

Username and Password

Name

Username and Password

Name

Username and Password

Name

Username and Password

Name

Username and Password

Name

Username and Password

Name

Username and Password

Name

Username and Password

Money I Owe to Others

(Keep your kneecaps intact and pay it, and tell them I say bye)

Person / Company Name

Contact Information

Documentation Location

Notes

Person / Company Name

Contact Information

Documentation Location

Notes

Person / Company Name

Contact Information

Documentation Location

Notes

Person / Company Name

Contact Information

Documentation Location

Notes

Additional Notes

Additional Notes, Instructions, and Wise Cracks

BANKING INFORMATION

Note: Please secure this document somewhere safe due to its sensitive information, (ideally in a safe, appropriately named).

Bank Name

Account Type and Number

Account Type and Number

Bank Online Web Address

Username and Password

Debit Card Number

Credit Card Number

CV and Password

Online Username and Password

Rewards

Notes / What I Love / Hate About This Bank

Bank Name

Account Type and Number

Account Type and Number

Bank Online Web Address

Username and Password

Debit Card Number

Credit Card Number

CV and Password

Online Username and Password

Rewards

Notes / What I Love / Hate About This Bank

Bank Name

Account Type and Number

Account Type and Number

Bank Online Web Address

Username and Password

Debit Card Number

Credit Card Number

CV and Password

Online Username and Password

Rewards

Notes / What I Love / Hate About This Bank

Safe Deposit Box

Bank Location

Box Number

Key Location

Contents (Such as Mouse Trap, Thumb Tacks, and Other Things to Swat / Stab Your Fingers)

Safe Deposit Box

Bank Location

Box Number

Key Location

Contents (Naughty Pics of You and Stuff)

Other Credit: Credit Cards, Line of Credit, Department Stores, Etc.

(Umm, you may be a tad shocked or annoyed by the balances, sorry ☹)

Name

Account Number

Online Website

Username and Password

Name

Account Number

Online Website

Username and Password

Name

Account Number

Online Website

Username and Password

Name

Account Number

Online Website

Username and Password

Name

Account Number

Online Website

Username and Password

Notes

Other Credit: Credit Cards, Line of Credit, Department Stores, Etc.

(Yup, there's more)

Name

Account Number

Online Website

Username and Password

Name

Account Number

Online Website

Username and Password

Name

Account Number

Online Website

Username and Password

Name

Account Number

Online Website

Username and Password

Name

Account Number

Online Website

Username and Password

Notes

Other Credit: Credit Cards, Line of Credit, Department Stores, Etc.

(...and more)

Name

Account Number

Online Website

Username and Password

Name

Account Number

Online Website

Username and Password

Name

Account Number

Online Website

Username and Password

Name

Account Number

Online Website

Username and Password

Name

Account Number

Online Website

Username and Password

Notes

Mortgage, Line of Credit, Loans

(Did you know 'mortgage' means 'until death'. What assholes.)

Mortgage Details

Bank / Lender

Contact Information

Account Number

Documentation Location

Second Mortgage Details

Bank / Lender

Contact Information

Account Number

Documentation Location

Third Mortgage Details

Bank / Lender

Contact Information

Account Number

Documentation Location

Other

Bank / Lender

Contact Information

Account Number

Documentation Location

Notes

Line of Credit Details

(Why the hell do they call it 'credit' when it's really 'debt'? Shouldn't it say 'Line of Debit'?)

Line of Credit

Bank / Lender

Contact Information

Account Number

Documentation Location

Line of Credit

Bank / Lender

Contact Information

Account Number

Documentation Location

Other

Bank / Lender

Contact Information

Account Number

Documentation Location

Other

Bank / Lender

Contact Information

Account Number

Documentation Location

Notes

Loans: Cars, Student Loan, Etc.

(Well, at least I qualified)

Bank / Lender _____

Contact Information _____

Account Number _____

Documentation Location _____

Bank / Lender _____

Contact Information _____

Account Number _____

Documentation Location _____

Bank / Lender _____

Contact Information _____

Account Number _____

Documentation Location _____

Bank / Lender _____

Contact Information _____

Account Number _____

Documentation Location _____

Bank / Lender _____

Contact Information _____

Account Number _____

Documentation Location _____

Notes _____

IMPORTANT DOCUMENTATION LOCATION

Note: The following documentation location is based solely on my memory; accuracy was dependent on hunger, stress or grumpy levels, and perhaps other mood altering options.

Will

Notes

Health Care Power of Attorney Papers

Notes

Passport

Notes

Birth Certificate

Notes

Social Security Card

Notes

Drivers Licence

Notes

Marriage Certificate

Notes

Tax Documents

Notes

Divorce Papers

Notes

Life Insurance

Notes

Health Insurance - Medical

Notes

Health Insurance Location – Dental

Notes

Health Insurance Location - Vision

Notes

Health Insurance Location – Other

Notes

Funeral Insurance

Notes

Vehicle Insurance #1

Notes

Vehicle Insurance #2

Notes

Vehicle Insurance #3

Notes

Home Owner Insurance

Notes

Rental Home Insurance

Notes

Children's Insurance #1

Notes

Children's Insurance #2

Notes

Children's Insurance #3

Notes

Other Family / Dependents Insurance

Notes

Pet Insurance #1

Notes

Pet Insurance #2

Notes

Storage Insurance #1

Notes

Storage Insurance #2

Notes

Additional Notes

Important Documents Location

Other

_____

Notes

Other

_____

Notes

Other

_____

Notes

Other

_____

Notes

Other

_____

Notes

Other

_____

Notes

Important Documents Location

(And Notes on Alternative Hiding Places Not Mentioned Above)

INSURANCE PROVIDER INFORMATION

Health Insurance – Primary Health (Ass Holes)

Company Name

Agents Name

Contact Information

HSA (Health Savings Account) Information

Health Insurance – Dental (Kiss My Assets)

Company Name

Agents Name

Contact Information

Notes

Health Insurance – Vision (Ya, I See You)

Company Name

Agents Name

Contact Information

Notes

Health Insurance – Medical #2 (I needed more, insurance makes me sick)

Company Name

Agents Name

Contact Information

Notes

Additional Notes

Life Insurance #1 (Lucky you)

Company Name

Agents Name

Contact Information

Notes

Life Insurance #2 (Even luckier!)

Company Name

Agents Name

Contact Information

Notes

Vehicle Insurance #1 (They all work, stop whining)

Company Name

Agents Name

Contact Information

Notes

Vehicle Insurance #2

Company Name

Agents Name

Contact Information

Notes

Vehicle Insurance #3 (Almost all that is)

Company Name

Agents Name

Notes

Home Owner Insurance (Pay attention, these matter)

Company Name

Agents Name

Contact Information

Notes

Rental Home Insurance

Company Name

Agents Name

Contact Information

Notes

Children's Insurance #1

Company Name

Agents Name

Contact Information

Notes

Children's Insurance #2

Company Name

Agents Name

Contact Information

Notes

Children's Insurance #3

Company Name

Agents Name

Contact Information

Notes

Other Dependents Insurance

Company Name

Agents Name

Contact Information

Notes

Pet Insurance #1 (Especially these)

Company Name

Vets Name

Contact Information

Notes

Pet Insurance #2

Company Name

Vets Name

Contact Information

Notes

Storage Insurance #1 (Good luck clearing it out, there's always next spring)

Company Name

Agents Name

Contact Information

Notes

Storage Insurance #2

Company Name

Agents Name

Contact Information

Notes

Funeral Insurance (Score!)

Company Name

Agents Name

Contact Information

Notes

Other Insurance (Omg, enough already with the insurance thing)

Company Name

Agents Name

Contact Information

Notes

Other Insurance

Company Name

Agents Name

Contact Information

Notes

Other Insurance

Company Name

Agents Name

Contact Information

Notes

Other Insurance

Company Name

Agents Name

Contact Information

Notes

Insurance Information – Notes

(And how much I hate the greedy Insurance Company SOB's)

MEDICAL INFORMATION

Serious shit, pay close attention

Health Care Power of Attorney

Name

Contact Information

Notes

Do Not Resuscitate Instructions Document Location

Notes

Organ Donor Instructions Document Location

Notes

Blood Type

Primary Care Physician

Name

Contact Information

Address

Notes

Medical Conditions

(Was it cuz of you stressing me TF out?)

Medications

(AKA big pharma residual income drug program. Congratulations on keeping the world sick for your greedy ass benefit. Karma's a bitch. Just you wait, ain't no pearly gate for you!)

Allergies, Food Sensitivity, and Reactions

(... to dumb ass humans)

If Incapacitated Please Honor These Wishes (Further Details in DNR Document)

(Man I'll be pissed, but just in case...)

Preferred Hospital

(No, I don't really prefer hospitals... I like my own bed)

Name

Contact Information

Address

Notes

Pharmacy

AKA Legalized Drug Pushers

Name

Contact Information

Address

Notes

Caregiver Company / Person #1

(I hope they're nice, if not use second option below)

Name

Contact Information

Address

Notes

Caregiver Company / Person #2

Name

Contact Information

Address

Notes

Medical Information - Notes

(Oh, don't even get me going on medical incompetence and doctors who think they're God. They can stick their needle right up their #@!*&!!)

DEPENDENTS INSTRUCTIONS OF CARE

My Dependents - My REAL ASSETS ☺

Name

Relationship

Contact Information

Personal Documentation Location

Health Conditions Documentation Location

Guardianship Instructions Documentation Location

Guardian Name

Contact Information

Primary Care Physician

Contact Information

Notes

My Dependents

Name

Relationship

Contact Information

Personal Documentation Location

Health Conditions Documentation Location

Guardianship Instructions Documentation Location

Guardian Name

Contact Information

Primary Care Physician

Contact Information

Notes

My Dependents

Name

Relationship

Contact Information

Personal Documentation Location

Health Conditions Documentation Location

Guardianship Instructions Documentation Location

Guardian Name

Contact Information

Primary Care Physician

Contact Information

Notes

Name

Relationship

Contact Information

Personal Documentation Location

Health Conditions Documentation Location

Guardianship Instructions Documentation Location

Guardian Name

Contact Information

Primary Care Physician

Contact Information

Notes

My Dependents

Name

Relationship

Contact Information

Personal Documentation Location

Health Conditions Documentation Location

Guardianship Instructions Documentation Location

Guardian Name

Contact Information

Primary Care Physician

Contact Information

Notes

My Dependents

Name

Relationship

Contact Information

Personal Documentation Location

Health Conditions Documentation Location

Guardianship Instructions Documentation Location

Guardian Name

Contact Information

Primary Care Physician

Contact Information

Notes

My Dependents – Pets (My Furry Kids and Free Therapy)

Name / Type of Pet_____

Name of Veterinarian_____

Contact Information_____

Address_____

_____

License, Insurance, and Documentation Location _____

_____

Health Conditions _____

_____

_____

Medications_____

_____

_____

Guardianship Instructions Documentation Location_____

_____

Guardian Name _____

Contact Information _____

General Instructions of Care – Food, Habits, Exercise, Sleep, and Other Needs

_____

_____

_____

_____

_____

Name / Type of Pet

Name of Veterinarian

Contact Information

Address

License, Insurance, and Documentation Location

Health Conditions

Medications

Guardianship Instructions Documentation Location

Guardian Name

Contact Information

General Instructions of Care – Food, Habits, Exercise, Sleep, and Other Needs

Name / Type of Pet_____

Name of Veterinarian_____

Contact Information_____

Address_____

_____

License, Insurance, and Documentation Location _____

_____

Health Conditions _____

_____

_____

Medications_____

_____

_____

Guardianship Instructions Documentation Location_____

_____

Guardian Name _____

Contact Information _____

General Instructions of Care – Food, Habits, Exercise, Sleep, and Other Needs

_____

_____

_____

_____

My Dependents – Notes

(Don't forget to feed the dog, do your homework, lock the door, and remember knowledge is power... so learn everything you can about vaccines, compound interest, and anything else that affects your wellbeing on every level.)

My Dependents – Notes

My Dependents – Notes

LOOSE ENDS TO TIE UP

Follow Up: Cancel, Close, Pay, Change of Name, Etc.

Example: Hydro, Electric, Phone, Cable, Internet, Storage, Credit Cards, Autopay, Banking...

(This is going to be a BITCH of a chore, good luck with that)

Company _____

Contact Information _____

Account Number _____

Username and Password _____

Notes _____

Company _____

Contact Information _____

Account Number _____

Username and Password _____

Notes _____

Company _____

Contact Information _____

Account Number _____

Username and Password _____

Notes _____

Company _____

Contact Information _____

Account Number _____

Username and Password _____

Notes _____

Company

Contact Information

Account Number

Username and Password

Notes

Company

Contact Information

Account Number

Username and Password

Notes

Company

Contact Information

Account Number

Username and Password

Notes

Company

Contact Information

Account Number

Username and Password

Notes

Company

Contact Information

Account Number

Username and Password

Notes

Company

Contact Information

Account Number

Username and Password

Notes

Company

Contact Information

Account Number

Username and Password

Notes

Company

Contact Information

Account Number

Username and Password

Notes

Loose Ends to Tie Up

Company _____

Contact Information _____

Account Number _____

Username and Password _____

Notes _____

_____

Company _____

Contact Information _____

Account Number _____

Username and Password _____

Notes _____

_____

Company _____

Contact Information _____

Account Number _____

Username and Password _____

Notes _____

_____

Company _____

Contact Information _____

Account Number _____

Username and Password _____

Notes _____

_____

Loose Ends to Tie Up Online: Email, Website, Hosting, Social Media, Banking, Amazon eBay, Memberships (No snooping!)

Company_____

Contact Information _____

Account Number_____

Username and Password_____

Notes _____

_____

Company_____

Contact Information _____

Account Number_____

Username and Password_____

Notes _____

_____

Company_____

Contact Information _____

Account Number_____

Username and Password_____

Notes _____

_____

Company_____

Contact Information_____

Account Number _____

Username and Password_____

Notes _____

_____

Loose Ends to Tie Up Online:

Company

Contact Information

Account Number

Username and Password

Notes

Company

Contact Information

Account Number

Username and Password

Notes

Company

Contact Information

Account Number

Username and Password

Notes

Company

Contact Information

Account Number

Username and Password

Notes

Loose Ends to Tie Up Online:

Company_____

Contact Information _____

Account Number_____

Username and Password_____

Notes _____

_____

Company_____

Contact Information _____

Account Number_____

Username and Password_____

Notes _____

_____

Company_____

Contact Information _____

Account Number_____

Username and Password_____

Notes _____

_____

Company_____

Contact Information _____

Account Number_____

Username and Password_____

Notes _____

_____

Loose Ends to Tie Up Online:

Company _____

Contact Information _____

Account Number _____

Username and Password _____

Notes _____

_____

Company _____

Contact Information _____

Account Number _____

Username and Password _____

Notes _____

_____

Company _____

Contact Information _____

Account Number _____

Username and Password _____

Notes _____

_____

Company _____

Contact Information _____

Account Number _____

Username and Password _____

Notes _____

_____

FINAL WISHES AND INSTRUCTIONS
I GET THE LAST WORD, YES, AS USUAL

(In all seriousness, if you don't follow this to the 'T', I'm going to come and visit you from beyond and scare the shit out of you. Would you prefer flickering lights, shit falling over, a voice in your ear, or missing car keys? I'll go with all of the above and then some...if you don't follow through!)

Final Wishes and Instructions

Final Wishes and Instructions

Final Wishes and Instructions

Final Wishes and Instructions

Final Wishes and Instructions

Messages to My Loved Ones

♥ This is a Personal Message for:

_____

_____

_____

_____

_____

_____

_____

_____

_____

_____

_____

_____

_____

_____

_____

_____

_____

_____

_____

♥ This is a Personal Message for:

_____

_____

_____

_____

_____

_____

_____

_____

_____

_____

_____

_____

_____

_____

_____

_____

_____

_____

_____

_____

♥ This is a Personal Message for:

♥ This is a Personal Message for:

_____

_____

_____

_____

_____

_____

_____

_____

_____

_____

_____

_____

_____

_____

_____

_____

_____

_____

_____

_____

♥ This is a Personal Message for:

♥ This is a Personal Message for:

♥ This is a Personal Message for:

♥ This is a Personal Message for:

Additional Notes / Customize

Notes

Notes

Notes

Notes

Notes

Notes

LAST WORDS

‌
_____

_____

_____

_____

_____

_____

_____

_____

_____

_____

_____

Signature

_____

Name and Date

_____

Made in United States
Troutdale, OR
07/11/2024

21166708R00073